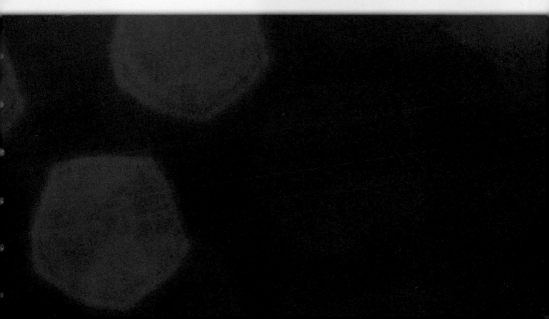

CONTEMPORARY LIVES

KATY PERRY

CHART-TOPPING SUPERSTAR

CONTEMPORARY LIVES

KATY PERRY

CHART-TOPPING SUPERSTAR

by Lisa Owings

Essential Library

An Imprint of Abdo Publishing | www.abdopublishing.com

www.abdopublishing.com

Published by Abdo Publishing, a division of ABDO, PO Box 398166,
Minneapolis, Minnesota 55439. Copyright © 2015 by Abdo Consulting
Group, Inc. International copyrights reserved in all countries. No part of this
book may be reproduced in any form without written permission from the
publisher. Essential Library™ is a trademark and logo of Abdo Publishing.

Printed in the United States of America, North Mankato, Minnesota
102014
012015

THIS BOOK CONTAINS
RECYCLED MATERIALS

Cover Photo: Shutterstock Images
Interior Photos: Shutterstock Images, 3; Rex Features/AP Images, 6–7, 21,
97; Steve Vas/Featureflash/Shutterstock Images, 11; Felipe Dana/AP Images,
13; Paul Smith/Featureflash/Shutterstock Images, 14–15, 96 (top); Splash
News/Corbis, 19; Jonathan Nowak/Dooley Productions/Shutterstock Images,
22–23, 100; Eric Draper/AP Images, 27; Ian White/Outline/Corbis, 33; S
Bukley/Shutterstock Images, 34–35, 53, 71, 95, 96 (bottom), 99; Stephane
Cardinale/People Avenue/Corbis, 43, 46–47; Jared Milgrim/Corbis, 44;
Sergio Moraes/Reuters/Corbis, 54–55; Matt Sayles/AP Images, 58, 64–65;
Chris Pizzello/AP Images, 63, 98 (top); Chris Young/Canadian Press/AP
Images, 73; Brian Friedman for iHeartRadio/The Hell Gate/Corbis, 74–75;
Mario Anzuoni/Reuters/Corbis, 78; J. Scott Applewhite/AP Images, 83;
AFLO/Nippon News/Corbis, 84–85; Dario Cantatore/Invision/AP Images, 88;
UNICEF, Kate Holt/AP Images, 90, 98 (bottom)

Editor: Susan E. Hamen
Series Designer: Emily Love

Library of Congress Control Number: 2014911370

Cataloging-in-Publication Data

Owings, Lisa.
 Katy Perry: chart-topping superstar / Lisa Owings.
  p. cm. -- (Contemporary lives)
Includes bibliographical references and index.
ISBN 978-1-62403-546-3
1. Perry, Katy, 1984- --Juvenile literature. 2. Singers--United States--
Biography--Juvenile literature. 1. Title.
782.42164092--dc23
[B]
                                                    2014911370

CONTENTS

Perry helped design the candy-inspired costumes and stage decorations that were a predominant theme for her 2011–2012 California Dreams Tour.

CHAPTER 1

"Just Love"

||||||||||||||||||||||||||||||||||||||||||||||||||||||||||||||||||||||||||||

C ell phone screens and camera flashes twinkled like stars against the dark São Paulo, Brazil, sky the night of September 25, 2011. A sea of 25,000 fans stretched from the stage to the horizon, all impatiently awaiting the moment pop sensation Katy Perry would step into the spotlight.[1] As they stood with their eyes and lenses trained on the set, three giant screens lit up. Screams of excitement burst into the air as a video showed Perry (and her cat, Kitty Purry) being transported from a humdrum, black-and-white life to a colorful, candy-coated fantasy world. As the film rolled and the fans roared, the flesh-and-blood star waited beneath the stage for her cue.

The São Paulo show came late in Perry's worldwide California Dreams Tour, and she was exhausted. Her relationship with her husband was suffering, and her emotions were becoming harder to hide. But this was the largest audience that had ever turned out to see one of her shows. Her Brazilian fans were the best, the most passionate, and she knew she couldn't disappoint them. Perry did a last-minute check of her hair, makeup, and costume. Then she stepped onto the platform that would lift her onto the stage. She took several deep breaths to collect herself, bringing all her focus to the performance she was about to give. Right on cue, she flashed a smile and struck a pose with her glittery microphone. Then the platform rose, propelling the star into the white light of the stage and the noise of the crowd.

Perry wanted her California Dreams Tour to be almost like a musical, so she filmed video segments that played between songs during her shows. The plot, she said, was "loosely based on my life, but a cartoon version."[2] Part *Wizard of Oz*, part *Alice in Wonderland*, and part Candy Land board game, the story began in a black-and-white world where Perry worked for a not-so-nice butcher. She longed for a better life with the cute baker boy she had met at the cupcake shop.

Then one night, she woke up to find Kitty Purry missing. Her search brought her into a wonderland of vivid colors and sugary candy. The videos followed her on her journey through this magical land in pursuit of Kitty and the baker boy. Together, the video segments and songs told a cohesive story throughout the show.

Brazil's KatyCats, as Perry called her fans, went wild the instant their idol appeared onstage. Her red-and-white peppermint-candy dress sparkled. Some of the candy-striped discs decorating it spun in hypnotizing harmony as she danced and sang. The first notes of Perry's hit single "Teenage Dream" were all but drowned out by screams. Then the entire crowd began singing along.

The smell of cotton candy wafted through the air as Perry moved across the candy-laden stage.

She passed through a forest of giant lollipops before descending stairs lined with candy canes. Iced mountains and cotton-candy clouds decorated the lower level of the stage, where Perry joined her whimsically costumed band, dancers, and backup singers. Perry waved to the crowd as she sang about having "no regrets, just love."[3] Her voice was almost as sugary sweet as the wonderland she had created for her audience.

Later in the show, a more serious Perry sang a soulful rendition of "The One That Got Away." Teary-eyed fans sang along and stretched their hands toward the stage. The song's storyline of a failed relationship brought Perry's emotions about her struggling marriage to the surface. By the end of the song, the crowd could sense she was barely holding it together. Perry tried to transition quickly to another song, but her fans started up a chant so loud she couldn't continue her show. "Katy, eu te amo!" cried thousands of Brazilians in unison. "Katy, we love you!"[4]

Perry's tears threatened to spill down her cheeks as her fans' cries washed over her. All the hardships of being on tour faded away in that moment. It was the culmination of everything Perry had wanted

Perry is known for her interaction with her fans, called KatyCats, and often takes selfies with a few lucky concertgoers.

since she was nine years old. Here she was, onstage in a sparkly dress, sharing her music and listening to 25,000 people chant her name. As Perry raised her hand to blow the crowd a heartfelt kiss, she knew her fairy-tale dreams had come true.

A SELF-MADE WOMAN

Perry did not have an easy road to fame. She was not discovered, handed a record deal, and molded into a pop star overnight. It was not luck but many years of hard work that made Perry's dream career a reality.

If Perry's life seems like a fairy tale, it most resembles the rags-to-riches story of Cinderella. Perry grew up in a deeply religious, low-income family. She went against her parents' religious beliefs and overcame financial difficulty to pursue her passion for pop music. Perry stayed true to her quirky personality, never gave up, and eventually made it to the top. But she didn't stop to rest once she got there.

> "I feel a real connection to fairy tales, and I think that in some ways, I live in a fairy tale."[5]
>
> —KATY PERRY

Perry would say she works harder today than she did before she got famous. She has a hand in every aspect of her brand and business, and those close to her admit her intuition is almost always right. She writes or cowrites all her songs, helps design sets and costumes for tours and performances, and stands up for herself when she

Perry's international success continues to grow as the pop star reinvents her style with each album.

doesn't feel her artistic vision is being respected. Despite differing views, she keeps her family involved in her journey. And she never takes her fans for granted. She knows they are responsible for her success, and she always goes out of her way to make them feel appreciated.

Underneath the wild costumes, colorful wigs, and false eyelashes is a talented singer-songwriter and a savvy businesswoman. Perry is also a real person who faces real struggles but never lets them slow her down. With her talent, determination, and perseverance, this pop princess has blazed her way to international fame, and she has no intention of relinquishing her hold on the world.

||||||||||

Despite her superstardom, Perry has remained close to her family.

CHAPTER 2

A Family on the Move

||||||||||||||||||||||||||||||||||||||||||||||||||||||

Even before Katy was born, her parents, Mary and Keith Hudson, had a feeling she would grow up to be extraordinary. Mary gave birth to her daughter Katheryn Elizabeth Hudson in Santa Barbara, California, on October 25, 1984. Katy was her parents' second child, and she grew up with an older sister and a

BLESSED NOT LUCKY

In the Hudson household, no one was allowed to mention the devil, even in a completely innocent context. The children had to call deviled eggs "angeled eggs," and Dirt Devil brand vacuum cleaners were not allowed in the house. Lucky Charms cereal was another no-no for Katy and her siblings. *Luck* sounded too close to *Lucifer*, another name for the devil. The Hudson children were always "blessed"—never "lucky"—when things were going their way.[2]

younger brother. The children were always very close, "like the Three Musketeers—actually, the Three Stooges," Katy said.[1] But their childhood was a little different from most.

Both Mary and Keith were born-again Christian ministers. They were strict parents with good intentions. Wanting to protect their children from unsavory influences, they censored everything from their music collections to their education. Katy's entire musical world consisted of hymns, gospel music, and other music with a Christian message. If she was lucky, she might get to listen to jazz artists Etta James or Billie Holiday. Any book other than the Bible was questionable, and television and movies had to stay G-rated. Katy's friends were church friends, and the summer camps and other activities she was involved in were all church activities. Everything in Katy's world revolved around the Christian faith.

Katy's education was also spotty due to her parents' lifestyle. They traveled around the country preaching to different congregations, so the

SISTERS

Katy has always been especially close to her older sister, Angela. Angela truly believed Katy had what it took to be a star, but the sisters never wanted fame to come between them. Angela recalled a pact they made when they were young: "We always kind of had this deal that, when she made it big, that I was going to work with her and we were going to be together."[3] They kept their promise to each other, and Angela was able to go on tour with Katy later in her career. She managed the meet-and-greets and other events with Katy's fans. During free time on tour, Katy and Angela would go exploring or do an activity together.

The sisters also supported each other in their personal lives. Katy credits Angela for helping her through the most difficult times in her marriage. In one of her songs, the singer thanks her sister for "keeping my head above the water."[4] Katy later put her own hardships aside to be a bridesmaid in Angela's wedding. And when Angela was in labor with her first child, Katy was there for her through the whole experience.

children were often pulled out of school. When they were able to attend, Katy and her siblings were placed in alternative schools that focused on religion. According to Katy, these schools did not offer a quality education. In fact, she says she still has trouble reading.

Money was tight more often than not. Katy's family lived on the donations her parents received from their congregations. If the people they preached to were not feeling generous, the family struggled to make ends meet. They relied on food stamps at times, and they scoured thrift stores and garage sales for other items they needed. Despite the money problems and constant moving, the children were more or less content. They didn't know any other way of living.

|||||||||||||||||||||||||||||||||||||||||||||||||||||

FROM FAMILY SINGER TO SERIOUS SONGWRITER

Between 1993 and 1994, when Katy was nine years old, her older sister, Angela, started singing lessons. Eager to copy everything her sister did, Katy started singing too. She would vie for her parents' attention by singing them songs she had taught

Katy's musical talents became apparent when she was a young girl.

herself. The strategy worked—her parents were impressed. They let Katy participate in the lessons, and soon she started singing in church. Katy's dad also paid her a few dollars to sing at dinners, family get-togethers, and other events. She loved the attention she got when she sang. "Everyone would drop what they were doing, and all eyes would be on me. It felt really powerful," she said.[5]

When Katy turned 11, her parents decided to start a more settled life in Santa Barbara. Katy began taking dance lessons at the local recreation center. She learned swing dancing from women dressed in vintage clothes, and the style really appealed to her. It would influence her unique fashion choices as she grew older.

For her thirteenth birthday, Katy asked for a guitar, and her love for music grew from there. She learned to accompany herself on guitar and started writing her own songs. She realized music could give her a platform to say whatever she wanted to say. It was an empowering realization.

After a while, Katy wanted to share her music with a wider audience than church and family. So she started performing at a Santa Barbara farmers' market. She liked to sing songs she had written herself to see how her audience would react. Those who liked her music would fill her guitar case with produce and maybe a few dollar bills. All her songs had a Christian message, and sometimes she would even try her hand at preaching.

Even if she had more avocados than money to show for it, Katy's voice was making a big impression. Her parents knew their daughter was more than just a pretty girl with a decent voice. They felt her talent was a gift from God, and they

Katy continues to demonstrate her guitar skills onstage during her concerts.

fully supported Katy in her dream of breaking into the Christian music industry.

By the time Katy was 15, she and her mother were making regular trips to Nashville, Tennessee, the heart of the Christian music scene. It was a scary experience for Katy, but she was determined to put herself out there. Her determination paid off when she caught the ear of a few industry veterans who took her under their wing. They helped her hone her songwriting skills, and Katy's goal of becoming a contemporary Christian music star seemed tantalizingly within reach.

||||||||||

After struggling in the Christian music industry, Katy eventually found success in mainstream pop music.

CHAPTER 3

Seeking Stardom

||||||||||||||||||||||||||||||||||||||||||||||||

Trying to make it in the Christian music industry was hard work, especially for a 15-year-old. Katy was trying to keep her grades up at her California high school while also raising her profile in Nashville. She was coming into her songwriting talent and giving performances whenever and wherever she could. It wasn't long before she caught the attention of a Christian record label. Katy signed with Red Hill Records in 2000 and quickly began recording her first album.

The self-titled album, *Katy Hudson*, was released in 2001. Its sound was alternative rock, and its theme was God, with the focus always on Katy's powerful vocals.

"For [Katy] to be making a Christian record was basically her becoming Michael Jackson in our family."[2]

—ANGELA HUDSON ON KATY'S CHRISTIAN RECORD

Initially, it seemed Katy had everything to be confident about. At 16, she had already produced an album that was getting positive attention. Katy toured across the United States to promote her album, and people were responding well to her music. However, her hopes of becoming the next Christian music star crumbled. Her record sold barely 200 copies, and by the end of 2001, her record label had gone bankrupt.[1] Katy's career had just begun, and it was already at a standstill.

NEW INSPIRATION

Disappointed but not defeated, Katy returned home to Santa Barbara. She got a job at an antique shop to make some extra money, and she still traveled to Nashville occasionally to meet with producers, offer her services as a backup singer, or give the occasional performance. But Nashville was becoming a dead end. Katy had to figure out a new strategy to get her career on track.

Also around this time, Katy started discovering secular music. She eagerly listened to her friends' music whenever she visited their homes, and she encouraged them to smuggle CDs to her. Some of her biggest influences were Freddie Mercury of Queen, Alanis Morissette, and Fiona Apple. She loved Mercury's theatricality and confidence, and she loved how Morissette and Apple wrote and sang so freely about their experiences as women. Katy recalled hearing "You Oughta Know" by Morissette for the first time and thinking,

> Wow. She just kind of let all of her thoughts and emotions come out. [She] didn't care what anyone else thought; she just did it completely honestly. Because of that, I just started singing

about everything I was going through as a young woman.[3]

With these artists as role models, Katy decided a bold change was necessary to rescue her career. She veered away from writing Christian songs and shifted her focus toward pop, even though it went against her family's values. Then one night while she was secretly watching cable music network VH1, big-time producer Glen Ballard came on the screen. He was talking about his work with Morissette on *Jagged Little Pill* (1995). Katy, already a fan of Morissette's, thought, "Well, that's a really good record. She speaks from my perspective. I want to make a record like that!"[4] And she wanted to make that record with Ballard.

So, true to her confident and determined nature, Katy drove to Los Angeles, California, with her dad to audition for the man behind her idol's success. One of her mentors in Nashville had pulled strings to get her an audition. Ballard simply recalls a young girl knocking on his door. Katy walked in, took out her guitar, and played him a song. "It blew me away," he said. "Right away I said, 'I want to sign you. You're it.'"[5]

Glen Ballard, Perry's future record producer, helped Alanis Morissette find success in 1995 with the album *Jagged Little Pill*.

The next day, Katy got a phone call from Ballard. He said, "I want you to move to Los Angeles. I want to help you fulfill your dreams."[6] She didn't need any more convincing. At 17, Katy left school, earned a high school equivalency certificate, and moved to Los Angeles on her own to pursue a career in mainstream music.

LIFE'S LESSONS IN LOS ANGELES

When Katy came to Los Angeles, she felt as if she were breaking free of the Christian world she had lived in as a child. She was flooded with new experiences, from going to dance clubs to wearing revealing clothing to meeting people of different sexual orientations. "I'm living life for the first time," she said of that period.[7]

As grateful and excited as she was to be working with Ballard, looking back, she said she was "a little entitled, a little bratty."[8] All of a sudden, she was living in Beverly Hills, California, working with a famous producer, and making a hefty income—she felt as if she had already made it. Still, she wasn't afraid of a little hard work. Under Ballard's guidance, Katy worked tirelessly to write songs, record demos, and film music videos. They both knew she needed to catch the attention of a record label that would be willing to produce her album. Luckily, Katy's work and Ballard's backing were good enough to get her signed to major record label Island Def Jam Music Group at the age of 17.

A NEW NAME, A NEW START

At this point, Katy Hudson decided to distinguish herself from similarly named actress Kate Hudson by taking her mother's maiden name. She officially became Katy Perry. She was also developing a sexier, more rock 'n' roll look. The new Perry worked with Ballard on her Island Def Jam album for more than a year. But the label just didn't seem to think she had what it took to be a star.

In 2003, Island Def Jam dropped Perry from their label. Perry was shocked. "I was in Beverly Hills with my new Jetta, thinking that my album was about to come out, and I was so excited," she

GLEN BALLARD

Glen Ballard is a songwriter and producer who has achieved success in a variety of musical genres. He has won six Grammy Awards and has worked with artists including Aretha Franklin, Michael Jackson, Barbra Streisand, Aerosmith, and Idina Menzel. Alanis Morissette's *Jagged Little Pill* was one of his most successful projects. He has also contributed to a number of movie soundtracks, including *The Polar Express* and *Charlotte's Web*, as well as musicals such as *Ghost the Musical*, based on the film starring Patrick Swayze and Demi Moore.

said in one interview.[9] In another, she tells the rest of the story:

> But it didn't last. I got dropped from my record label. And the Jetta was impounded. And I couldn't pay my bills. I suddenly heard no more often than yes.[10]

Perry was disheartened, but she still had Ballard's support, and the two started looking for the next opportunity. They found it at Columbia Records in 2004. After reviewing Perry's now-extensive body of work, Columbia signed Perry to their label. But they weren't quite sure what to do with her or how to market her. In the end, they decided to team her up with powerhouse production trio the Matrix. This group of songwriters and producers included Lauren Christy, Graham Edwards, and Scott Spock. They had a reputation for producing huge hits for the likes of Avril Lavigne, Britney Spears, and Jason Mraz. In 2004, the Matrix was working on their first album as a band, and they were looking for vocalists. Perry was one of the two singers chosen to front the Matrix's band. It seemed she was finally being set up for success.

Perry soon came to realize, though, that the Matrix's vision was a lot different from hers. They wanted Perry to be more like Avril Lavigne or other artists who had enjoyed recent success. Perry didn't want to be like other artists. She just wanted to be herself. This caused some friction between Perry and the Matrix, but ultimately she was willing to go along with the Matrix's demands in hopes that it would help her gain momentum in the industry.

Perry recorded with the Matrix until the album was almost complete. In anticipation of the album's release, music magazine *Blender* interviewed Perry and called her "the next big thing."[11] Again, the excitement of this achievement began to build. But again, the label put the brakes on the project at the last minute. The Matrix didn't feel their album was coming together as planned, so they didn't release it. And even though Perry was still on the label,

SMALL VICTORIES

Perry's early career was not all disappointment. One of her early songs, "Simple," was chosen for the soundtrack of *The Sisterhood of the Traveling Pants* in 2005. It is a popular film based on a book about a group of girls coming of age. Columbia Records released the movie soundtrack shortly before the film came out in June.

Columbia proved unwilling to promote her as a solo artist.

Ballard introduced her to manager Bradford Cobb in hopes that he could help steer her in a better direction. Cobb believed in Perry from the moment she cartwheeled into his office and landed in the splits. He said of their experience with Columbia Records:

> Columbia was never really willing to embrace Katy's vision. . . . Here was this ambitious young woman with a clear picture of who she was and the willingness to work hard, and Columbia just wouldn't put her in the driver's seat.[12]

Finally, in 2006, Columbia dropped her. This time, Perry was devastated. Her income disappeared, her car got impounded again, and she was nearly ready to give up and head back to Santa Barbara. She no longer knew who she was as a person or as a musician. On top of all that, people were telling her she was damaged goods, that no other label would want her. Despite her struggles, Perry found a way to make ends meet and auditioned for gigs every chance she got. She started writing for herself again, and she played her

In 2004, Perry experienced a short-lived run as a member of a recording group when her record label teamed her up with the Matrix.

songs at the Hotel Café and other places around Los Angeles. Perry found that when she stayed true to herself, her audience tended to believe in her. It helped her get back on the path toward believing in herself.

||||||||||

Despite early struggles with record labels, Perry didn't lose faith in herself and her own style.

CHAPTER 4
"I Kissed a Girl"

||||||||||||||||||||||||||||||||||||||||||||||||||||||||||||||||||||||||||||||||||||||||||||

omeone else from Columbia
Records believed in Perry
too. Publicist Angelica
Cob-Baehler had been a fan of Perry's
from the beginning. She felt so strongly
that Columbia had mistreated Perry
that she left the record label, and she
stole Perry's files and took them with
her. When Cob-Baehler landed a new

position at Capitol Records, she encouraged the label to consider signing Perry.

Capitol Records CEO Jason Flom agreed to meet with Perry. He was immediately impressed by her presence, her determination, and her talent. Flom decided to give her a chance. He signed her to the label in 2007. Even better, he wasn't going to turn Perry into a copycat artist. He believed in Perry's vision, and he was ready to let her take charge of her own destiny.

CONTROVERSIAL HITS

Because Perry had been writing and recording material for the past several years, she already had most of what she needed to release a record. But Capitol felt she still lacked a couple of truly radio friendly hits. They partnered her with songwriter and producer Dr. Luke, who worked with her to write "I Kissed a Girl" and "Hot N Cold" for the album.

In November 2007, Perry celebrated her first milestone at Capitol Records. She released a digital extended play (EP) with the track "Ur So Gay" as well as a cover and another song co-written by Perry. "Ur So Gay" got a lot of attention, mainly because of its controversial nature. Many listeners felt the song portrayed a negative view of gay people. Perry insisted the song was just poking fun at her metrosexual ex-boyfriend—it was not to be taken seriously, and it was certainly not meant to offend gay people.

Despite the questionable lyrics, "Ur So Gay" certainly had its fans. In April 2008, just before Perry's full album was scheduled to be released, pop superstar Madonna said during a radio interview that it was her current favorite song. "You have to hear it," she said. "It's so good."[1]

"I can't believe [Madonna] knew my first and last name and she gave me such a great shout-out. It's one of those things . . . she really knew everything and I was so impressed that she knew me. . . . I'm a new artist. I'm nobody. I'm just starting out and she has her finger on the pulse of what's going on and that's very cool."[2]

—KATY PERRY ON MADONNA

Perry was shocked and thrilled that Madonna had even heard of her. And needless to say, Madonna's endorsement earned Perry lots more attention. Adding to that was celebrity gossip blogger Perez Hilton's posts about Perry. He was already sold on Perry and felt she had "the whole package."[3]

In the midst of all the media-generated buzz, Perry released the lead single from her new album, "I Kissed a Girl," on April 28. With a chorus of "I kissed a girl and I liked it / The taste of her cherry ChapStick," the song was about exploring sexuality.[4] It proved no less controversial than "Ur So Gay," and Perry's parents were initially disappointed in the subject matter. But no one could deny the song was catchy, and its taboo nature made it extra appealing. It was an instant hit and soon climbed to Number 1 on the *Billboard* Hot 100 chart, where it would stay for seven weeks.[5] "I Kissed a Girl" also reached Number 1 in more than 20 other countries.[6] Perry's launch to stardom was well underway.

ONE OF THE BOYS

Perry's album *One of the Boys* came out on June 17, 2008. Other hit singles on the album included breakup ballad "Thinking of You," and energetic earworms "Hot N Cold" and "Waking Up in Vegas." The album did well, though reviews ran the gamut. One praised the album, "Not since *Jagged Little Pill* has a debut album been so packed with hits."[7] Another blasted it, "If you've got even a passing interest in actually enjoying a record, don't buy this one."[8]

Perry didn't have time to dwell on the negative reviews. Three days after her record came out, she was on the road for the Warped Tour 2008, a traveling music festival that lasted throughout the summer. It was a wild ride, and the male- and

FROSTING FALL

October 2008 found Perry at the MTV Latin America Awards in Mexico. At the end of her performance of "I Kissed a Girl," she belly flopped into a giant pink cake, playfully throwing frosting at the crowd. The frosting made the stage so slick, however, that Perry took a tumble. She tried to get up, then took a few more falls, seemingly for comic effect as the crowd laughed. Finally, Perry crawled out of the danger zone and was helped off the stage.

punk-rock-dominated tour was not her usual scene, but Perry fit right in. She tweaked her songs and her onstage persona to be a little edgier, and fans couldn't help but crowd surf to her punkified version of "I Kissed a Girl."

> "[Warped Tour] was one of the hardest things I've ever done because it was literally show after show after show, no showers . . . we were all crammed into this bus and it was hot . . . but I really held my own and I learned how to keep the attention of an audience . . . and I learned the art of connecting with my audience, and now it's really still all about that."[9]
>
> —KATY PERRY ON THE WARPED TOUR

Perry was also kissing a certain boy on the tour. Her boyfriend at the time was Travie McCoy, lead singer of the rap rock band Gym Class Heroes. They had met at a New York recording studio in 2006. The two started dating the following year and continued their relationship long distance while Perry was working in California. The Warped Tour finally gave them the chance to spend some quality time together. When the summer was over, it was that much harder to return to opposite coasts.

||||||||||||||||||||||||||||||||||||||||||||||||||||||||||||||||||||

AWARDS SEASON

Luckily, Perry had plenty to distract her from her loneliness. She was thrilled to be asked to perform at the MTV Video Music Awards (VMAs) in September. The newly famous singer arrived with her friend Miley Cyrus at the venue dressed in a pinup-worthy vintage outfit. She then donned a short white romper with a glittery, peelable banana at the neckline to perform a cover of Madonna's hit "Like a Virgin" as well as her own "I Kissed a Girl." Perry had also been nominated for a number of awards, including Best New Artist, though she didn't win any that evening.

Shortly after the VMAs, Perry's manager told her MTV had invited her not only to perform at but also host their Europe Music Awards (EMAs) show in November. It was a huge honor, and Perry jumped at the opportunity. Her natural charisma, wit, and charm—not to mention her quirky fashion sense—were on full display. Perry opened the show with a big production of "I Kissed a Girl." A group of dancers dressed as cheerleaders chanted Katy Perry's name. They circled the stage as Perry appeared atop a platform rising from the center. Dressed in football gear and straddling a giant tube of ChapStick, Perry launched into her Number 1 hit. As she hosted the show, her several costume changes included a colorful carousel dress. A carnival-tent pattern decorated the top of the dress, and the skirt spread into a rotating model of a carousel, complete with circus characters and animals. Later, in a half-tuxedo, half-wedding dress outfit, she got the crowd jumping with a performance of "Hot N Cold." To top off the night, she picked up an award for Best New Act.

And the year wasn't over yet. In December, despite missing the call due to losing her phone at a concert venue, Perry found out she had been nominated for a Grammy Award. She was up for Best Female Pop Vocal Performance, along with Pink, Adele, and other inspiring artists. Perry couldn't wait to find her phone so she could listen to all the messages of congratulations. "It'll be like Christmas!" she said.[10]

Over-the-top costumes and theatrical performances have always been a mainstay of Perry's concerts.

Perry's success strained her relationship with fellow musician Travie McCoy.

After all the excitement of the past year, Perry looked forward to spending time with her boyfriend over the holidays. The two traveled to Mexico for what was surely meant to be a relaxing vacation. But instead of bringing them closer, the time together only highlighted their differences. McCoy was full of self-doubt and insecurity about Perry's success, and Perry had neither the time nor the desire to slow down her career for the sake of a rocky relationship. As the New Year approached, reports began circulating that the couple had broken up. Perry wanted to focus on her career. She had finally achieved the pop stardom she had always dreamed of, and no one was going to stop her now.

||||||||||

During the 2008 MTV Europe Music Awards in Liverpool, England, Perry descended from the ceiling on a large banana.

CHAPTER 5

Hello Katy

‖‖‖

Perry was excited to see what 2009 had in store for her. It was setting up to be a big year. Perry would be starting her first headlining tour on January 23, so preparations were in full swing. It had also been announced that she would be performing at the Grammy Awards in

February. When asked what to expect from her Grammy night show, she said, "Fruit."[1]

And fruit is, indeed, what viewers got. Perry was lowered in a giant banana to a stage crowded with other massive fruits. Behind her, multiple screens flashed colorful images of fruits. And Perry's dress was covered in glittery fruit decorations. The singer's quirky visuals, strong voice, and fun choreography made her umpteenth performance of "I Kissed a Girl" feel fresh. It hardly seemed to matter that she didn't win an award that night.

PRE-GRAMMY NERVES

Perry admitted she was nervous for her first Grammy performance. "I have this little sick-to-my stomach feeling. I think it's a healthy feeling," she said.[2] On the red carpet, she made light of her worries, joking about getting stuck in the banana pod in which she would be lowered to the stage. Perry also talked about her odd choice of good luck charms. She shared a dressing room with fellow young musicians Miley Cyrus and Taylor Swift. She asked for a lock of hair from each, put bows on them, and carried them in her purse. The charms seemed to work!

ON THE ROAD

Fruit was also a theme during Perry's worldwide Hello Katy Tour. And cats. And, as always, clothes. Her set designer—"the guy who creates stages for Madonna," Perry said—based the tour's backdrop on the album cover for *One of the Boys*.[3] It featured a patch of faux grass, a white picket fence, a mailbox, and supersized ornamental flamingos.

Perry appeared under a pink lit-up heart in a sparkly pink outfit with a short, ruffled skirt. Accompanied by a band dressed in white, the star belted out songs from her album—along with a couple of covers—as her fans sang along. During one song, she invited a lucky member of the audience to dance with her onstage. During another, she playfully tossed beach-ball-sized inflatable strawberries into the crowd. Perry also showed off her guitar skills during stripped-down ballads "Thinking of You" and "Lost." Between songs, Perry chatted with the crowd and regaled them with funny stories.

For the show's finale, a giant cat's head with glowing eyes moved onto the stage. Perry changed into a pink jumpsuit with kitty ears and a tail.

The last song was "I Kissed a Girl," and it never failed to get the audience members moving and screaming the lyrics. Perry alternated between dancing with a giant inflatable tube of cherry ChapStick and bouncing around onstage. Near the end of the song, she jumped into the crowd, surfing upright and still singing. After shouting the last line into her glittery microphone, Perry bent down through dozens of outstretched arms to kiss a girl in the crowd.

The ten-month-long tour was grueling, but Perry enjoyed performing and interacting with her fans in Asia, Australia, North America, and Europe. She tried hard to stay healthy so she could make as many of her tour dates as possible. And even though she was busy with her world tour, Perry still found time to promote her album through interviews and additional performances wherever she went.

A WHIRLWIND ROMANCE

During the summer of 2009, Perry took a break from touring to film a cameo appearance for the film *Get Him to the Greek*. It was a comedy

On August 4, 2009, Perry performed as the opening act for rock band No Doubt. Perry had long admired lead singer Gwen Stefani. She sang a few of the biggest hits from her album, including "Hot N Cold" and "Thinking of You," saving "I Kissed a Girl" for last. Later, Perry joined No Doubt onstage to help them sing their last song, "Stand and Deliver."

costarring British comedian and actor Russell Brand. For Perry's scene, she had to kiss Brand, and she definitely liked it. "On the way down the stairs after the scene, I was hopping like a bunny," she said. "I hop like a bunny when I'm happy—I get a bit childlike. He gives me the Christmas Eve jitters."[4] The scene was later cut from the movie, but Perry brushed off the slight with her usual sense of humor.

The pair didn't reconnect again until the MTV VMAs in September. Brand was hosting the show, and Perry would be introducing him with a glitzy opening performance of Queen's "We Will Rock You." Apparently, sparks were flying in rehearsals, with the two relentlessly and flirtatiously teasing each other. At the end of the show, Brand declared, "Katy Perry didn't win an award and she's staying in the same hotel as me, so she's going to need a shoulder to cry on. So in a way, I'm the real winner tonight."[5] It was a bit of a bold move, but shortly after the show, rumors were flying about the couple's budding romance. Celebrity gossip had it that Perry and Brand were spotted kissing that night at an after party.

The relationship between Perry and Brand got serious quickly. Later that month, the busy couple made time for an exotic getaway to Thailand. By the time Perry's twenty-fifth birthday rolled around in late October, the two had made their relationship public. Brand helped Perry celebrate in style with a *Willy Wonka and the Chocolate Factory*–themed bash. Partygoers were instructed to wear white (Perry chose a white dress and Oompa Loompa nail decals), not knowing they would leave the party splattered with paint. True to the theme, there were candies and sweets galore, including a birthday cake that triggered a food fight. Perry's family and friends, including Taylor Swift and Perez Hilton, were having so much messy fun the fire marshals shut things down early.

In December, Brand whisked Perry off to Asia once again over the holiday season. This time, the

Perry created a lot of buzz when she began dating
Russell Brand, who was nine years older.

destination was India. The pair enjoyed visiting
the Taj Mahal and experiencing Indian cuisine and
culture. On New Year's Eve, Brand asked Perry to
marry him. She said yes. The two had fallen deeply
in love, and they couldn't wait to spend their
lives together.

||||||||||||

The year 2010 brought much radio airplay for Perry's new *Teenage Dream* songs.

CHAPTER 6

Setting Off
Fireworks

||||||||||||||||||||||||||||||||||||||||||||||||||

The newly engaged Perry kicked off 2010 with another Grammy nomination for Best Female Pop Vocal Performance, this time for "Hot N Cold." When she heard about the repeat honor, she joked, "Again? Jeez!"[1] But of course, Perry was thrilled that her *One of the Boys* album was still carrying so much momentum from the previous year. "It was encouraging," she said of the nomination.[2]

For her second Grammy appearance, Perry chose a close-fitting backless dress decorated with gold flowers and sequins. This time, she didn't feel like an out-of-place newcomer. She finally felt accepted by the people and the industry that had shut her out for so many years, and she knew she was on the right path in her career. Perry's fiancé came with her to the event. Although the pop artist again went home without a Grammy, she had fun presenting an award and celebrating her friend Taylor Swift's win for Album of the Year. After the show, the star tweeted, "Tonight was lovely; don't think I'll be sleepin' on 2010."[3]

TEENAGE DREAM

True to her word, Perry was already hard at work on her new album. She wanted to create a summery pop record that would get people moving and also reflect the new experiences she'd had since *One of the Boys*. For the first song on the new album, she was inspired by Jay Z's New York tribute anthem "Empire State of Mind," featuring

Alicia Keys. Perry felt the West Coast deserved a song too, and the California native was just the artist to deliver it. She teamed up with a few other songwriters to get the lyrics right, and she flattered rapper Snoop Dogg into being the featured artist on the track.

The song, "California Gurls," was released in May 2010, and it quickly skyrocketed to Number 1 on the *Billboard* Hot 100. In fact, it was the fastest-rising single by a Capitol Records artist in more than 40 years.[4] "California Gurls" proved to be the perfect summertime hit, remaining at the top of US charts for six weeks and also reaching Number 1 in several other countries.[5]

CANDYFORNIA

For her "California Gurls" music video, Perry chose a Candy Land board game theme. It shows Perry moving as a game piece through a world where everything is made of candy and sweets. Featured artist Snoop Dogg rolls sugar-cube dice to determine how the game progresses. Some of Perry's over-the-top costumes in the video include a cupcake bikini top and a bra that shoots whipped cream. She also appears in a silvery-purple wig atop a cotton candy cloud.

Perry and rap legend Snoop Dogg performed "California Gurls" at the MTV Movie Awards in 2010.

The next single from the album was the title track, "Teenage Dream." Perry wrote the song in her hometown of Santa Barbara, taking herself back to her early teen years. She collaborated with songwriter Bonnie McKee and others to create a song that captured the giddiness of falling in love for the first time. The lyrics had to be rewritten several times before everyone felt good about the end result, but the time they spent on the song paid off. Released in July, the song climbed to Number 1 in the following weeks.[6]

On August 24, 2010, Perry released the much anticipated *Teenage Dream*. Again, reviewers had mixed feelings about the album. While acknowledging the catchy melodies, many complained the lyrics felt shallow or over the top. BBC reviewer Al Fox wrote that *Teenage Dream* has "intelligence, individuality, and character in abundance. But all too often it's caked in

PURRFUME

In November 2010, Perry revealed the results of her newest business venture. She introduced her first fragrance, Purr, a tribute to her love of cats. Perry said she had been working on the perfume for more than a year to make sure it was the best representation of her. She was proud of the fruity, floral scent she came up with. Perry also had a hand in designing the purple cat-shaped bottle.

To create advertisements for her new scent, Perry was photographed in a pink and purple rubber cat suit. Her product first came out in a London department store, where Perry spent hours mingling with fans and signing perfume boxes. Purr was a success, and it remained the number-one-selling fragrance on the market for more than two months.[7]

dollar-store body glitter and choked by feather boas."[8] He suspected something greater lay beneath the sugary glitz.

For Perry's fans, the sugary glitz proved more than enough. The album debuted at Number 1, with sales of close to 200,000 records in a single week.[9] Three other songs on the album soon followed the first two singles to Number 1. They included Perry's inspirational anthem "Firework," catchy alien love song "E.T.," and dance party hit "Last Friday Night (T.G.I.F.)." That made Perry the first woman and the second artist ever to produce five Number 1 hits on the same album. The first musician to achieve this feat? "King of Pop" Michael Jackson with his 1987 album, *Bad*.[10] The sixth single from *Teenage Dream*, "The One That Got Away," also made it into *Billboard*'s top five.[11]

Perry spent much of the rest of the year promoting her album and spending time with her fiancé. In September, she filmed a segment for *Sesame Street* in which she sang about playing dress-up with Elmo, to the tune of "Hot N Cold." However, parents who previewed the segment felt Perry's dress was too low-cut. *Sesame Street* producers decided not to air the segment, but the controversy still brought Perry plenty of publicity. Later that month, the singer performed as the musical guest on sketch comedy show *Saturday Night Live*. She also appeared in a skit, wearing an Elmo T-shirt and poking fun at her *Sesame Street* scandal.

In October, Perry released the music video for her favorite song from *Teenage Dream*, "Firework." The song assures listeners who find themselves going through a difficult time that they are unique and irreplaceable, and that things will get better. Perry dedicated the video to the It Gets Better Project, which supports lesbian, gay, bisexual, and transgender (LGBT) youth. "Everyone has the spark to be a FIREWORK," was her message to the LGBT community.[12] The song would go on to win the MTV VMA for Video of the Year in 2011.

KATHY BETH TERRY

For Perry's "Last Friday Night" music video, she played the stereotypically nerdy girl Kathy Beth Terry. Dressed in out-of-date clothes, broken glasses, and a headgear, Perry brought humor and charm to the character, who could barely remember the crazy party she'd just been to. The popularity of Kathy Beth Terry proved Perry didn't need sex appeal to sell music.

AN INDIAN WEDDING

The biggest event in October 2010 was Perry's wedding to Brand. The two returned to India, where they had gotten engaged, for a six-day celebration fit for royalty. They were careful to keep the festivities as private as possible. Family and friends were treated to wildlife safaris as well as live music and dancing. Perry and Brand immersed themselves in Indian culture, wearing traditional clothing, featuring Indian music in their celebrations, and participating in Indian wedding traditions such as henna tattooing. On the Friday before the wedding, the couple threw a

IT GETS BETTER

The It Gets Better Project began in 2010 in response to a rise in LGBT youth suicides, especially offering support to youth who were being bullied. The project posted inspirational online videos to assure LGBT youth that things would get better, that there is always hope for the future, and that they are not alone. The project grew over the years, collecting video submissions from President Barack Obama, comedian Ellen DeGeneres, and many other public figures. The project also offers a supportive online community and, in 2011, it published the book *It Gets Better: Coming Out, Overcoming Bullying, and Creating a Life Worth Living*.

Perry and Brand escaped the paparazzi for their private wedding in India.

Bollywood-themed bash that involved acrobats and Indian drums. Perry wore a red sari.

The wedding ceremony took place at a luxury resort within a wildlife reserve known for its tiger population. An Indian news agency said the traditional wedding procession included elephants, camels, and horses. Perry reportedly wore a lacy gray Elie Saab dress for at least part of the ceremony. Surrounded by flower garlands, traditional music, and loved ones, a longtime friend of Perry's family pronounced the couple husband and wife on October 23.

||||||||||

At the 2011 Grammys, Perry treated fans to exclusive footage of her wedding.

CHAPTER 7

California Dreams

IIIIIIIIIIIIIIIIIIIIIIIIIIIIIIIIIIIIIIIIIIIIIIII

ove was still in the air on Valentine's eve 2011, when Perry found herself back at the Grammys once again. This time she was honored with multiple nominations, including one for Album of the Year. Accompanied by her 90-year-old grandmother and her husband, Perry walked the red carpet in an angelic white Armani gown complete with feathery wings.

Perry also performed a love-themed medley at the Grammy Awards. In a sparkling white minidress adorned with hearts and a long train, she sat on a swing with the fabric of her train draped over the back. After she had sung the first verses of "Not Like the Movies," a song from her *Teenage Dream* album, the swing rose and the train of her dress was pulled into a giant projector screen. Never-before-seen footage of Perry's wedding to Brand was projected onto the fabric as she continued singing. Then she was lowered back to the stage, and she immediately launched into a rendition of "Teenage Dream" dedicated to "all the Valentine lovers."[1] In the end, Perry didn't win any of the awards for which she had been nominated. But it had been a special evening for her.

SUGAR AND SPICE AND EVERYTHING NICE

After celebrating her first Valentine's Day with husband Brand, Perry was gearing up for another yearlong world tour. She wanted her California Dreams Tour to be bigger than ever, telling fans:

I hope that it's going to engage all of your senses: sight, sound, smell, taste, touch. I'm really excited about . . . making a massive production of it. . . . I want it to be ten times better than when I was on tour last.[2]

"The press is just not your friend when it comes to marriage. That's why we didn't sell the pictures of our wedding, and we got offered millions of dollars for them. . . . I felt the moment [at the Grammys] was right and not forced. Russell and I had time to savor our moment privately first and then share it with people when we were ready, and *not* for a paycheck. I loved the idea, because I thought it was beautiful and artistically accompanied the song I wrote for him. Plus, it was Valentine's eve!"[3]

—KATY PERRY ON SHOWING HER WEDDING FOOTAGE DURING HER GRAMMY PERFORMANCE

Preparations were rushed, but Perry knew she had to make time to get in shape and to perfect all the details before her team went on the road. She likened getting ready for the tour to training

During the summer of 2011, Perry was able to try her hand at voice acting. She supplied the voice of Smurfette in the animated film *The Smurfs*, based on a comic about small blue creatures. Perry enjoyed the experience, saying the role felt like a natural extension of her vocal skills and cartoony personality. The singer took the opportunity seriously and spent some time tweaking her voice to fit her character. She described the voice of Smurfette as "my voice and a bag of rocks, with a pinch of sugar."[4] The film proved unpopular outside of its target audience of young children, but *The Smurfs 2*, in which Perry was also involved, followed in 2013.

for the Olympics. She had to work out hard to build enough stamina for the long performances she would be giving almost every night. There was also a strict diet to follow, voice lessons to attend, dances to learn, and e-mails about the show to address.

Approximately a week before the tour commenced, intense rehearsals started in Los Angeles. Designers scurried to put costumes together for everyone who would be onstage, working out kinks in any of Perry's outfits that had moving parts. Stage crews set up props and other visual effects, including lasers, whipped-cream guns, giant lollipops, and harnesses to lift dancers into the air. Perry, her dancers, and the rest of the team soldiered through many late nights trying to get every movement, every costume change, and every note exactly right. Finally, the show got on the road with seven buses full of people and 16 trucks full of equipment.

The California Dreams Tour was all about sweets, from the dancers' delectable costumes to the candy-coated stage to the dancing gingerbread men. Perry's almost-edible outfits were the most creative. Her costumes included a dress with spinning peppermint candies, one with a tiered skirt decked out in cupcakes, and another that transformed her into an ice cream sundae. Perry managed at least 15 costume changes per show, including eight during "Hot N Cold" alone. The piped-in scent of cotton candy and whipped-cream cannons that frosted the audience completed the sweet spectacle. For "Peacock," Perry donned a jewel-toned leotard with a feather tail that trailed on the floor until she flipped it up behind her. Flashing lights and dancing lasers created an otherworldly look for "E.T." During "Firework," real fireworks exploded over the stage. And the "California Gurls" finale involved a soaked audience, beach balls, and confetti. Candy and cupcakes aside, the music was the star of the show. Perry sang all the songs from *Teenage Dream*, plus her biggest hits from her previous album. She also included a few covers, such as Rihanna's "Only Girl (in the World)" and Whitney Houston's "I Wanna Dance with Somebody."

Perry gave 124 performances across North America, South America, Europe, Asia, and Australia. More than $175,000 in proceeds from the North American leg of the tour went to charities, including those supporting animal rights and children's health.[5] Thanks to Perry's vision, the tour was a huge success. It was soon sold out around the world. Perry knew this was not something to be taken for granted. She said, "To say that you had a sold-out arena tour, in the first five years of your career . . . it's not supposed to happen like that."[6] During the MTV EMAs in November, Perry beat out Lady Gaga to claim the award for Best Live Act. Parts of the tour were also filmed for Perry's upcoming documentary— particularly her November show at Staples Center

In 2011, Perry put her colorful personality to work as the voice of Smurfette in the film *The Smurfs*.

in Los Angeles. The film was set to be released in 2012.

SOMETHING'S GOT TO GIVE

Even as Perry was enjoying the heights of pop stardom, her marriage to Brand was suffering. It was difficult for the couple to spend time together while Perry was often touring on the opposite side of the world from Brand.

An exhausted Perry would fly for hours to see Brand at least every two weeks in an effort to keep their marriage strong. She felt Brand was not showing the same dedication to their relationship. She thought he seemed resentful of her success at times. The comedian was also pushing for children even though Perry did not feel ready. She felt one of the reasons Brand was so keen on kids was that he wanted to shift Perry's focus from her career to her home life. Regardless of the true circumstances,

SATURDAY NIGHT LIVE

In December 2011, Perry got to show off both her comedy and her singing skills as the host of *Saturday Night Live* (*SNL*). After a monologue poking fun at her outlandish costumes, she went on to do hilarious impressions of fellow artists Florence Welch and Christina Aguilera. She also did an impression of Pippa Middleton, sister of the Duchess of Cambridge, and participated in a digital short with *SNL* veteran Andy Samberg.

Young girls dressed as characters from Perry's videos accompanied Perry at the 2012 Much Music Video Awards in Toronto.

their marriage collapsed. On New Year's Eve 2011, two years after their engagement and just 14 months after their wedding, Brand text-messaged Perry to ask for a divorce.

||||||||||

Despite undergoing personal heartache, Perry has maintained a busy touring schedule.

CHAPTER 8
"Wide Awake"

||||||||||||||||||||||||||||||||||||||||||||||||||||||||||||||||||||||||||

erry was shocked and humiliated by the callous way Brand ended their short marriage. She spent the next two weeks in a deep depression, eating junk food and canceling her scheduled appearances. At one point, Perry wasn't sure she could go on living. Then she found a way to channel her grief into material for her new album. Although at first she thought her songs would revolve around blame and revenge, she found herself turning inward and focusing on healing and self-improvement.

Perry was also gathering her strength to finish the California Dreams Tour. She had two more dates scheduled. Tweeting her excitement, she took off for Asia in late January 2012. She gave her all for her final performances in Indonesia and the Philippines, and despite a security glitch before the last show, she delivered exactly what her fans had been waiting for.

BOMB SCARE

Perry had been looking forward to her final California Dreams performance in the Philippines. But her excitement turned to fear when the show was delayed due to a bomb threat. Security dogs trained to find bombs had been searching the area where the concert would take place. They seemed to have caught the scent of a bomb inside a backpack in Perry's dressing room. Perry was evacuated from the scene in an armored car. She later recalled, "I think I started crying at one point because I was just so overwhelmed."[1] But in the end, it turned out it was chicken that had attracted the dogs to the backpack, not a bomb. "We call it the chicken bomb now," Perry joked after the incident.[2]

MOVING ON

Perry had little downtime before her next big performance at the Grammy Awards. On February 12, Perry strolled the red carpet in a frothy, pale blue, lace-and-sequin gown that complemented her blue hair. However, come performance time, she ditched the good-girl look.

Green and blue lights danced across the stage as Perry sang the opening to "E.T." Suddenly, her voice cut out and everything went dark. "We lost power," said a voice over the speakers.[3] Then the outline of a box became visible, and Perry was crouched inside wearing a bodysuit that resembled battle armor with blue sunglasses and her blue hair untamed. She sang the first lines of her newest and not-yet-released song, "Part of Me," a cappella. When the band started playing, she stood up and punched through the glass enclosure. Flames rose across the stage during the chorus, then briefly went out as Perry sang:

> So you can keep the diamond ring / It don't mean
> nothing anyway / In fact you can keep everything
> / Except for me.[4]

Perry performs at the 2012 Grammy Awards.

It seemed clear Perry was making a public statement about her divorce—she had moved on, tapped her inner strength, and would continue to sparkle for herself and her fans.

BUSINESS IS BOOMING

Perry didn't want to wait until she completed a new record to release some of the new songs she had been working on. So in March, Perry rereleased *Teenage Dream* as *Teenage Dream: The Complete Confection*. The rerelease featured three new songs, including "Part of Me" and a few remixes. Perry had written one of the new tracks, "Wide Awake," to accompany the end credits of an autobiographical film she was working on. The song was about waking up from her teenage dream, coming to terms with her divorce, and ending up stronger for the experience. Critics were disappointed with the lack of new material on the album, but Perry argued that the few bonus tracks were the perfect ending to *Teenage Dream* and a way of giving her fans insight into her feelings about the divorce.

Perry's film, *Katy Perry: Part of Me*, came out in early July 2012. The documentary followed Perry during her California Dreams Tour. Perry wanted her movie to be as honest as possible, so she included footage of her being emotionally vulnerable and without makeup and costumes. Also woven into the film was the story of Perry's childhood and the ups and downs of her career. The most visually stunning aspect of the movie was the concert footage, which cleverly tied into the plot and showed Perry in all her audiovisual glory. The film was shot in 3-D, making its visuals that much more impressive.

> There's some scenes [in *Katy Perry: Part of Me*] that I know people will screenshot and be like, 'Oh, she looks like a fat cow with zits.' But I put those in there because that's a part of me, that's reality, and I'm OK with that now. It's been a process of learning it's OK, and I'm accepting of my own skin, but I think it's important for young kids to see that you don't have to be perfect in order to achieve your dreams."[5]
>
> —*KATY PERRY ON LETTING HER IMPERFECTIONS SHOW*

Making the movie in the first place was a gamble. Perry put $2 million of her own money into it, against her business manager's best judgment. Predictably, the film was a hit among Perry's fans. But many of those reluctant to board the Katy Perry train also seemed to enjoy it, or at

BY THE GRACE OF GOD

During her pop career, Perry has distanced herself from her Christian upbringing. But she still relies on God to get her through tough times. After her divorce, Perry wrote a song called "By the Grace of God." The lyrics tell how her faith got her through the depression and suicidal thoughts she experienced. Perry also has Jesus's name tattooed on her wrist. She says it reminds her of her roots. And although she no longer identifies as Christian, she feels her belief in God keeps her grounded and is still an important part of her life.

least respect it. *Katy Perry: Part of Me* earned more than $7 million in its opening weekend and went on to earn more than $30 million worldwide. It lagged behind some other films in the genre, including the previous year's *Justin Bieber: Never Say Never*. Still, it proved a good marketing tool and career choice for Perry. In fact, by the end of 2012, Perry was named one of the highest-paid women in music.

LIVING AND LOVING

Later in July, Perry and Brand's divorce was finalized after the six-month waiting period required in California. It didn't take Perry long to find love again. In early August, she was spotted out on the town with fellow musician John Mayer, and rumors of romance were swirling. Over the next few months, it became clear they were an item. Things seemed to be getting serious. In November, Mayer traveled with Perry to her hometown for a romantic getaway.

Fortunately, Perry's new love interest seemed to be compatible with her career. On November 30, Perry's success led to her accepting *Billboard's* Woman of the Year award. She delivered an eloquent, funny speech in which she thanked the many women who had inspired her, including her peers, family, and fans. In an interview with the magazine, she mentioned she had already begun work on a new album. "I have lots of songs and ideas. I know exactly the record I want to make

HOLIDAY DREAMS

For Perry and Mayer, holiday festivities included spending time with patients at a local hospital in association with the Dream Foundation. The Dream Foundation is a wish-granting organization for terminally ill adults and their families. Photos of the visit showed the couple doing holiday crafts, posing for pictures, and engaging in other activities with patients who were unable to spend the holidays at home.

After her heartbreaking divorce, Perry found happiness again with singer John Mayer.

next. I know the artwork, the coloring, and the tone, but I'm not in the studio yet," she said.[6]

Before she began work in earnest, she was ready for a break. "I need to live so I have something worth singing about," she said.[7] In December, Perry became more open about who she was spending her free time with. She and Mayer appeared as an official couple at a Rolling Stones concert and other events while traveling together on the East Coast. Then the couple celebrated the holidays together with Perry's family in Santa Barbara.

⁏⁏⁏⁏⁏⁏⁏⁏⁏

Perry is greeted by adoring fans in Japan.

CHAPTER 9

Prismatic Perry

‖‖

Perry's 2013 started off low-key, wrapping up her *Teenage Dream* era with one final awards season. There were still no Grammy Awards in sight, but she scooped up an armful of People's Choice Awards for Favorite Female Artist,

Favorite Pop Artist, Favorite Music Video, and Favorite Music Fan Following.

Then it was into the studio to work on the new album. She stayed tight-lipped about it, but she did say this record was going to be different from anything she had done before. "It will be an evolution," she said. "I'm not going to try and replicate what I did last."[1] Perry's excitement about her work shone through in interviews, and her fans were equally excited about what was to come.

In April 2013, Perry had the opportunity to visit Madagascar, an island off the coast of Africa, with children's rights organization UNICEF. She helped highlight the need for foreign aid to provide underprivileged children with nutritious food, education, health care, and safe living conditions. The trip was life changing for Perry, and it also inspired at least one of the songs on her new record.

Perry's relationship with Mayer seemed a bit less solid than her career. The couple had allegedly broken things off in March, but they were back on by summer. In July, Mayer publicly declared his love for Perry during a concert. He dedicated a song to her and talked about how she helped him get through surgery on his vocal cords.

> "In less than one week here in Madagascar, I went from crowded city slums to the most remote villages, and my eyes were opened wide by the incredible need for a healthy life—nutrition, sanitation, and protection against rape and abuse—which UNICEF is stepping in to help provide."[2]
>
> —KATY PERRY ON HER TRIP TO MADAGASCAR

ROARING—AND ROMANCE

The same month, a golden truck rolled through the streets of Los Angeles emblazoned with the name of Perry's new album: *Prism*. Perry unleashed her first single from the album in August. "Roar" showed the shift that had taken place since Perry's divorce. No longer grieving a failed relationship, her new single was all about empowerment—and a catchy pop melody. Inspiration from Helen Reddy's "I Am Woman" and Survivor's "Eye of the Tiger" are clear in the chorus: "I got the eye of the tiger, a fighter / Dancing through the fire / 'Cause I am

Perry broke out a new fashion statement with her boxing-inspired costume for "Roar."

a champion / And you're gonna hear me roar."[3] The song was yet another instant hit for Perry. It quickly climbed to Number 1 on the *Billboard* Hot 100.[4]

The star's performance of "Roar" later in August in Brooklyn, New York, made the song even more appealing. Dressed as a boxing champion with a fighting ring for a stage and dancers dressed in workout gear, Perry showed her fans a fiercer side of her. She even jumped rope in the middle of the song and still had the energy to belt out a last repeat of the chorus. The singer had officially shed her cupcakes-and-candy image.

Perry was also the featured artist on a song Mayer released that month. "Who You Love" is ultimately a love song, though it acknowledges some of the challenges Perry and Mayer had faced in their relationship. Mayer partially inspired the next single for *Prism*, "Unconditionally." Perry's other inspiration for the song was her trip to Madagascar, where she saw a special kind of love that had nothing to do with social power or material possessions.

ROAR!

To promote her new single "Roar," Perry posted a couple of teaser videos online. The first showed Perry burning the blue wig that had become a signature look on the California Dreams tour. Then the release date of the single popped up in tiger print. In the second video, Perry attends a funeral for the peppermint-candy-dress essence of *Teenage Dreams*. In the "Roar" music video, Perry further sheds her girly-girl image. She becomes stranded in the jungle and gradually changes from a privileged, helpless traveler to a survivor and a jungle queen.

Perry interacts with children in Madagascar while on a UNICEF relief mission.

The full album was released in October. It had a multifaceted sound, with more introspective lyrics. Some felt *Prism* was not as much fun as *Teenage Dream*. Others appreciated Perry's more mature approach to the record. *Telegraph* reviewer Helen Brown said, "[Perry] sounds like a woman, and an artist, who's finally found herself."[5] *Prism* debuted at Number 1 on the *Billboard* 200, with 286,000 records sold in the first week.[6] These were record-breaking sales for Perry.

Meanwhile, Perry and Mayer seemed closer than ever, with the press speculating they might soon be engaged. It seemed the rumors could be true when Perry started making public appearances with jewels on her left ring finger.

Perry ended the year on a humanitarian note, with UNICEF naming her as the organization's newest goodwill ambassador. The star's April trip to Madagascar had inspired her to become more involved with UNICEF. She was thrilled to use her celebrity to shed light on the needs of children around the world.

SINGLE AND SUCCESSFUL

Shortly after the New Year, Perry and Mayer broke up again. Rumor had it Mayer had been seeing other women. And perhaps the prospect of another lengthy world tour—similar to the one that had contributed to the collapse of Perry's marriage— had also been weighing heavily on the relationship.

After the successful release of her third album, Perry announced she would be devoting much of 2014 to another world tour. She promised it would be "less cartoony but just as dynamic as always, and it will be a feast for your eyes."[7]

She also hinted that the format of the tour would allow her to connect more with fans.

With no romantic ties, Perry was ready to give 100 percent for her Prismatic World Tour. It kicked off in Europe in May 2014. Perry delivered what she had promised—another massive production with a less unified theme that allowed for even more stunning visual effects. Her stage was shaped like a prism, with its point cutting through the center of the audience so Perry could get close to as many fans as possible. The show was divided into several segments, each with a different theme built around *Prism* songs plus all the fan favorites from previous albums.

The show opened with a giant, brightly lit prism closing like a clamshell and then opening

COPYING GAGA?

In a tweet after the start of Perry's Prismatic World Tour, avant-garde pop artist Lady Gaga implied that Perry had copied some of her ideas. "It looks like green hair and mechanical horses are the thing now," Gaga posted online.[8] Perry did wear a green wig and ride a fake horse during parts of her Prismatic World Tour, after Gaga had ridden a similar horse down an awards-show red carpet and dyed her hair green. Perry never responded to the apparent insult.

to reveal Perry in a glow-in-the-dark dress and ponytail. More dazzling, prismatic light effects took her through "Roar" and the rest of the songs in the first segment. For the next, she emerged as Cleopatra atop a golden horse. The prisms changed to pyramids, and her dancers were dressed in ancient Egyptian garb. The song "E.T." included acrobats dancing on and dangling from a rotating diamond-shaped cage. Other segments featured cats, sunflowers, butterflies, and neon lights. For "Birthday," a bevy of balloons appeared to lift Perry into the air and over the audience. The finale was "Firework." The audience was asked to put on special glasses before Perry appeared in a firework-inspired dress. Pyrotechnics and prismatic firework displays awed fans before Perry was again swallowed up by her prism.

MUCH MORE TO COME

Even with the rest of her Prismatic World Tour ahead of her, Perry has been looking to the future. She has no intention of slowing down her career and is already thinking about her next album. Surprisingly, she might stray from

her tried-and-true pop sound. She said in
one interview:

> As I inch toward my 30s, I think my fourth record
> will be more of an acoustic guitar album. That's
> where I started when I was first discovered by
> Glen Ballard and got my first record deal.[9]

Rumors were circulating during the tour that
she might come out with a new album as early as
2015, but Perry had yet to reveal her plans.

In her personal life, Perry has always been
a romantic. She hopes to find love with a true
teammate who will support her dreams and
aspirations. Eventually, she wants to start a family,
but she doesn't feel ready quite yet. Right now, her
focus is on her career and her fans.

Like light through a prism, Perry is a woman
of many colors. She is passionate about writing
songs, making music, and sharing her vision
with the world. She has an intuitive feel for how
to manage her business and lead her team. She
loves being in love, and she always makes time for
her family, friends, and fans. When she can, she
gives back to communities in need. With Perry's
brand of ambition and drive, there is little doubt

The future looks promising for Perry, pictured with her arms full of trophies at the 2011 MTV Video Music Awards.

her fans will see many more facets of her, from addictive hit songs to outrageous fashion choices to head-over-heels love—always with no regrets.

||||||||||

TIMELINE

1984

1993–1994

1997

Katheryn Elizabeth Hudson is born in Santa Barbara, California, on October 25.

Perry starts singing in church and at other family functions.

Perry receives a guitar for her thirteenth birthday and begins writing her own songs.

2007

2008

2009

Perry is signed to Capitol Records, where she is finally able to pursue her own vision.

Perry's first pop record, *One of the Boys*, is released on June 17.

On January 23, Perry begins her first world headlining tour, the Hello Katy tour.

2001	2003	2006
Perry's first album, *Katy Hudson*, is released under Christian record label Red Hill Records.	Island Def Jam Music Group drops Perry from the label after more than a year of work.	Columbia Records drops Perry, again, after a significant amount of time and work.

2009	2009	2010
Perry meets comedian Russell Brand while filming a cameo for *Get Him to the Greek*.	On December 31, Perry and Brand get engaged.	Perry's second pop album, *Teenage Dream*, is released on August 24.

TIMELINE

2010

Perry becomes the second artist ever to produce five Number 1 hits on the same album.

2010

Perry marries Brand in India on October 23.

2011

Perry embarks on her yearlong California Dreams Tour.

2012

Perry's autobiographical film, *Katy Perry: Part of Me*, hits theaters in July.

2012

On November 30, Perry is named *Billboard*'s Woman of the Year.

2013

In April, Perry travels to Madagascar with UNICEF, a children's rights organization.

2011

Brand texts Perry to ask for a divorce on December 31.

2012

At the Grammy Awards in February, Perry gives a powerhouse performance that shows she has begun to move on from the divorce.

2012

Perry rereleases *Teenage Dream: The Complete Confection* in March with new songs and remixes.

2013

In October, Perry releases her third pop album, *Prism*.

2013

Perry becomes one of UNICEF's goodwill ambassadors in December.

2014

In May, Perry begins her Prismatic World Tour.

GET THE SCOOP

FULL NAME

Katheryn Elizabeth Hudson

DATE OF BIRTH

October 25, 1984

PLACE OF BIRTH

Santa Barbara, California

PARENTS

Mary and Keith Hudson

MARRIAGE

Russell Brand (October 2010–December 2011)

ALBUMS

Katy Hudson (2001), *One of the Boys* (2008), *Teenage Dream* (2010), *Prism* (2013)

TOURS

Warped Tour (2008), Hello Katy Tour (2009), California Dreams Tour (2011–2012), Prismatic World Tour (2014)

SELECTED AWARDS

- Won the MTV EMA for Best New Act in 2008
- Won the MTV EMA for Best Live Act in 2011 (California Dreams Tour)
- Won the MTV VMA for Video of the Year in 2011 ("Firework")
- Won the American Music Award for Special Achievement in 2011
- Won the *Billboard* Music Award for Woman of the Year in 2012
- Won the People's Choice Awards for Favorite Female Artist, Favorite Pop Artist, Favorite Music Video, and Favorite Music Fan Following in 2013
- Won the NRJ Music Awards for International Song of the Year ("Roar") and International Female of the Year in 2013

PHILANTHROPY

Katy Perry has been closely involved with UNICEF and has also worked with the It Gets Better Project and the Dream Foundation.

"I think it's important for young kids to see that you don't have to be perfect in order to achieve your dreams."

—KATY PERRY

GLOSSARY

anthem—An uplifting song that becomes popular primarily among a specific group of people.

Billboard—A music chart system used by the music recording industry to measure record popularity and sales.

charisma—A magnetic charm or appeal.

chart—A weekly listing of songs or albums in order of popularity or record sales.

crowd surfing—Being passed from person to person above a large crowd.

culmination—The high point or climax of something.

debut—A first appearance.

documentary—A film about real people and events.

endorsement—A public approval or support for a product as a way to get other people to buy it.

extended play (EP)—A musical release with more than one song or track, but not enough for an album.

genre—A category of art, music, or literature characterized by a particular style, form, or content.

headliner—The main performer at a concert.

intuition—An instinctive feeling that causes someone to act in a certain way.

pop—A commercial or popular style of music.

producer—Someone who oversees or provides money for a play, television show, movie, or album.

record label—A brand or trademark related to the marketing of music videos and recordings.

rendition—A performance or interpretation of something, often a piece of music.

single—An individual song distributed on its own over the radio and other mediums.

stamina—The ability to do something physically or mentally difficult for a long period of time.

venue—The place where a concert or other event is held.

whimsical—Playful or fanciful, usually in an amusing way.

ADDITIONAL RESOURCES

SELECTED BIBLIOGRAPHY

"Katy Perry." *Newsmakers*. Vol. 1. Detroit: Gale, 2011. *Biography in Context*. Web. 13 May 2014.

Katy Perry: Part of Me. Dirs. Dan Cutforth, Jane Lipsitz. Paramount Pictures, 2012. DVD.

Wiig, Kristen. "Katy Perry." *Interview Magazine*. Interview Magazine, 2 Mar. 2012. Web. 11 June 2014.

Woods, Vicki. "Beauty and the Beat: Katy Perry's First *Vogue* Cover." *Vogue*. Condé Nast, 20 June 2013. Web. 11 June 2014.

FURTHER READINGS

Ehrlich, Ken. *At the Grammys! Behind the Scenes at Music's Biggest Night*. New York: Hal Leonard Books, 2007. Print.

Marsico, Katie. *Lady Gaga: Pop Singer & Songwriter*. Minneapolis, MN: ABDO, 2012. Print.

Summers, Kimberly Dillon. *Katy Perry: A Biography*. Santa Barbara, CA: Greenwood, 2012. Print.

WEBSITES

To learn more about Contemporary Lives, visit **booklinks.abdopublishing.com**. These links are routinely monitored and updated to provide the most current information available.

PLACES TO VISIT

Capitol Studios
1750 Vine Street
Los Angeles, CA 90028
323-871-5001
http://www.capitolstudios.com
Check out the iconic Capitol Records Tower, where Katy
Perry and other famous artists record their albums.

The Hotel Café
1623 North Cahuenga Boulevard
Los Angeles, CA 90028
323-461-2040
http://www.hotelcafe.com
Visit the small Los Angeles venue where Katy Perry often
performed before she became a star.

SOURCE NOTES

CHAPTER 1. "JUST LOVE"

1. Luiis Perry. "Katy Perry Concert Candy: South America." *YouTube.* YouTube, 19 Sept. 2012. Web. 31 Aug. 2014.

2. Jocelyn Vena. "Katy Perry Reveals Tour Will Have 'Smell-O-Vision.'" *MTV News.* Viacom, 27 Jan. 2011. Web. 31 Aug. 2014.

3. *Katy Perry: Part of Me.* Dir. Dan Cutforth and Jane Lipsitz. Paramount Pictures Corporation, 2012. Film.

4. Ibid.

5. Ibid.

CHAPTER 2. A FAMILY ON THE MOVE

1. Rose Apodaca. "Katy Perry: The Interview." *Harpers Bazaar.* Hearst Communications, 3 Nov. 2010. Web. 31 Aug. 2014.

2. Vanessa Grigoriadis. "Sex, God & Katy Perry." *Rolling Stone.* Rolling Stone, 19 Aug. 2010. Web. 31 Aug. 2014.

3. *Katy Perry: Part of Me.* Dir. Dan Cutforth and Jane Lipsitz. Paramount Pictures Corporation, 2012. Film.

4. "By the Grace of God." *Katy Perry.* Capitol Records, 2014. Web. 31 Aug. 2014.

5. Noam Friedlander. *Katy Perry.* New York: Sterling, 2012. Print. 18.

CHAPTER 3. SEEKING STARDOM

1. Noam Friedlander. *Katy Perry.* New York: Sterling, 2012. Print. 25.

2. *Katy Perry: Part of Me.* Dir. Dan Cutforth and Jane Lipsitz. Paramount Pictures Corporation, 2012. Film.

3. Ibid.

4. CBSNEWS. "'All Access': Katy Perry." *CBS.* CBSNEWS, 4 Feb. 2009. Web. 31 Aug. 2014.

5. *Katy Perry: Part of Me.* Dir. Dan Cutforth and Jane Lipsitz. Paramount Pictures Corporation, 2012. Film.

6. CBSNEWS. "'All Access': Katy Perry." *CBS.* CBSNEWS, 4 Feb. 2009. Web. 31 Aug. 2014.

7. *Katy Perry: Part of Me.* Dir. Dan Cutforth and Jane Lipsitz. Paramount Pictures Corporation, 2012. Film.

8. Lynn Hirschberg. "Katy Perry (In Any Language)." *W Magazine.* Condé Nast, 22 Oct. 2013. Web. 31 Aug. 2014.

9. Vanessa Grigoriadis. "Sex, God & Katy Perry." *Rolling Stone.* Rolling Stone, 19 Aug. 2010. Web. 31 Aug. 2014.

10. Lynn Hirschberg. "Katy Perry (In Any Language)." *W Magazine.* Condé Nast, 22 Oct. 2013. Web. 31 Aug. 2014.

11. Noam Friedlander. *Katy Perry*. New York: Sterling, 2012. Print. 38–39.

12. "Katy Perry." *Newsmakers*. Vol. 1. Detroit: Gale, 2011. *Biography in Context*. Web. 13 May 2014.

CHAPTER 4. "I KISSED A GIRL"

1. Noam Friedlander. *Katy Perry*. New York: Sterling, 2012. Print. 61.

2. Ibid.

3. Jeremy Leeuwis. "Katy Perry to Release Ur So Gay." *MUSICREMEDY*. MUSICREMEDY, 29 Oct. 2007. Web. 31 Aug. 2014.

4. "I Kissed a Girl." *Katy Perry*. Capitol Records, 2014. Web 31 Aug. 2014.

5. *Katy Perry: Part of Me*. Dir. Dan Cutforth and Jane Lipsitz. Paramount Pictures Corporation, 2012. Film.

6. Noam Friedlander. *Katy Perry*. New York: Sterling, 2012. Print. 65.

7. "One of the Boys." *Billboard*. Nielsen Business Media, 21 June 2008. Web. 31 Aug. 2014.

8. Ibid.

9. Linzy Pi. "MTV Unplugged Interview – Katy Perry." *YouTube*. YouTube, 1 March 2011. Web. 31 Aug. 2014.

10. WENN. "Perry Missed Out on Grammy Nod News." *Contactmusic. com*. Contactmusic.com, 4 Dec. 2008. Web. 31 Aug. 2014.

CHAPTER 5. HELLO KATY

1. James Montgomery. "Katy Perry Talks about Her Split from Travis McCoy . . . Sort Of." *MTV News*. Viacom, 9 Jan. 2009. Web. 31 Aug. 2014.

2. Noam Friedlander. *Katy Perry*. New York: Sterling, 2012. Print. 81.

3. Cortney Harding. "Katy Perry Ready for First Headlining Tour." *Billboard*. Nielsen Business Media, 23 Jan. 2009. Web. 31 Aug. 2014.

4. Amy Spencer. "Katy Perry (She Kisses Boys, Too!)." *Glamour Magazine*. Condé Nast, n.d. Web. 31 Aug. 2014.

5. Jocelyn Vena. "Katy Perry and Russell Brand: A Timeline of Their Love." *MTV News*. Viacom, 6 Jan. 2010. Web. 31 Aug. 2014.

CHAPTER 6. SETTING OFF FIREWORKS

1. Noam Friedlander. *Katy Perry*. New York: Sterling, 2012. Print. 107.

2. Ibid.

3. Ibid.

4. James Montgomery. "Katy Perry's 'California Gurls' Makes History in Rise to #1." MTV News. Viacom, 9 June 2010. Web. 31 Aug. 2014.

SOURCE NOTES CONTINUED

5. Randy Lewis. "'California Gurls' Versus 'California Girls': Brian Wilson, Make Love Chime In on Katy Perry's Hit Single." *LA Times Music Blog*. LA Times, 20 July 2010. Web. 31 Aug. 2014.

6. Silvio Pietroluongo. "Katy Perry's 'Teenage Dream' Dethrones Eminem on Hot 100." *Billboard*. Nielsen Business Media, 8 Sept. 2010. Web. 31 Aug. 2014.

7. Noam Friedlander. *Katy Perry*. New York: Sterling, 2012. Print. 127.

8. Al Fox. "Katy Perry Teenage Dream Review." *BBC*. BBC, n.d. Web. 31 Aug. 2014.

9. Keith Caulfield. "Katy Perry's 'Prism' Set for No. 1 Debut on Billboard 200 Chart." *Billboard*. Nielsen Business Media, 23 Oct. 2013. Web. 31 Aug. 2014.

10. Gary Trust. "Katy Perry Makes Hot 100 History: Ties Michael Jackson's Record." *Billboard*. Nielsen Business Media, Inc. 17 Aug. 2011. Web. 31 Aug. 2014.

11. "Katy Perry's 'Teenage Dream' Yields Sixth Hot 100 Top Five Hit." *Billboard*. Nielsen Business Media, 14 Dec. 2011. Web. 31 Aug. 2014.

12. Scott Zumwalt. "Katy Perry Dedicates New Video 'Firework' to It Gets Better Project." *It Gets Better Project*. It Gets Better Project, 28 Oct. 2010. Web. 31 Aug. 2014.

CHAPTER 7. CALIFORNIA DREAMS

1. Ilovepopmusic. "Katy Perry Live Grammys." *Vimeo*. Vimeo, n.d. Web. 31 Aug. 2014.

2. Noam Friedlander. *Katy Perry*. New York: Sterling, 2012. Print. 137.

3. "Katy Perry on Her Religious Childhood, Her Career, and Her Marriage to Russell Brand." *Vanity Fair*. Vanity Fair, 23 May 2011. Web. 2 Sept. 2014.

4. Kristy McCormack. "'It's Like My Voice with a Pinch of Sugar' Says Katy Perry on Playing Smurfette." *Express*. Northern and Shell Media Publications, 29 Nov. 2013. Web. 2 Sept. 2014.

5. "Katy Perry Celebrates over $175K Raised for Charity on Her California Dreams Tour through Tickets-for-Charity." *Santa Barbara Independent*. Santa Barbara Independent, 14 Dec. 2011. Web. 2 Sept. 2014.

6. Noam Friedlander. *Katy Perry*. New York: Sterling, 2012. Print. 137.

108

CHAPTER 8. "WIDE AWAKE"

1. Kristen Wiig. "Katy Perry." *Interview Magazine.* Interview Magazine, n.d. Web. 2 Sept. 2014.

2. Ibid.

3. Katy Perry HK. "Katy Perry – E.T. / Part of Me (Live at 54th Grammy 2012)." *Vimeo.* Vimeo, n.d. Web. 2 Sept. 2014.

4. Ibid.

5. James Montgomery. "Katy Perry Accepts Her 'Own Skin' in 'Part of Me' Film." *MTV News.* Viacom, 20 June 2012. Web. 2 Sept. 2014.

6. Gail Mitchell. "Katy Perry Q&A: *Billboard's* Woman of the Year 2012." *Billboard.* Nielsen Business Media, 8 Dec. 2012. Web. 2 Sept. 2011.

7. "Katy Perry Won't Rush New Album: 'I Know Exactly the Record I Want to Make Next.'" *Capital FM.* Capital FM, 1 Dec. 2012. Web. 2 Sept. 2014.

CHAPTER 9. PRISMATIC PERRY

1. Billboard. "Katy Perry on Being *Billboard's* 2012 Woman of the Year." *YouTube.* YouTube, 29 Nov. 2012. Web. 2 Sept. 2014.

2. "Katy Perry Teams Up with UNICEF and Visits Children in Madagascar." *UNICEF.* UNICEF, 7 Apr. 2013. 2 Sept. 2014.

3. "Roar." *Katy Perry.* Capitol Records, 2014. Web. 31 Aug. 2014.

4. Gary Trust. "Katy Perry Dethrones Robin Thicke Atop Hot 100." *Billboard.* Nielsen Business Media, 4 Sept. 2013. Web. 2 Sept. 2014.

5. Helen Brown. "Katy Perry, Prism, Review." *Telegraph.* Telegraph Media Group, 17 Oct. 2013. Web. 2 Sept. 2014.

6. Keith Caulfield. "Katy Perry's 'PRISM' Shines at No. 1 on Billboard 200." *Billboard.* Nielsen Business Media, 30 Oct. 2013. Web. 2 Sept. 2014.

7. Christina Garibaldi. "Katy Perry's Tour Will Be a 'Feast for Your Eyes' . . . And Your Instagram." *MTV News.* Viacom, 11 Nov. 2013. Web. 2 Sept. 2014.

8. Sierra Marquina. "Lady Gaga Tweets Jab at Katy Perry for Having Green Hair, Riding a Fake Horse During Her Prismatic World Tour." *US Magazine.* Wenner Media, 8 May 2014. Web. 2 Sept. 2014.

9. "Katy Perry on Her Future: 'I'll Probably Turn into More of a Joni Mitchell.'" *NME.* IPC Media, 30 Sept. 2013. Web. 2 Sept. 2014.

INDEX

INDEX CONTINUED

ABOUT THE AUTHOR

Lisa Owings has a degree in English and creative writing from the University of Minnesota. She has written and edited a wide variety of educational books for young people. Lisa lives in Andover, Minnesota, with her husband and a small menagerie of pets.